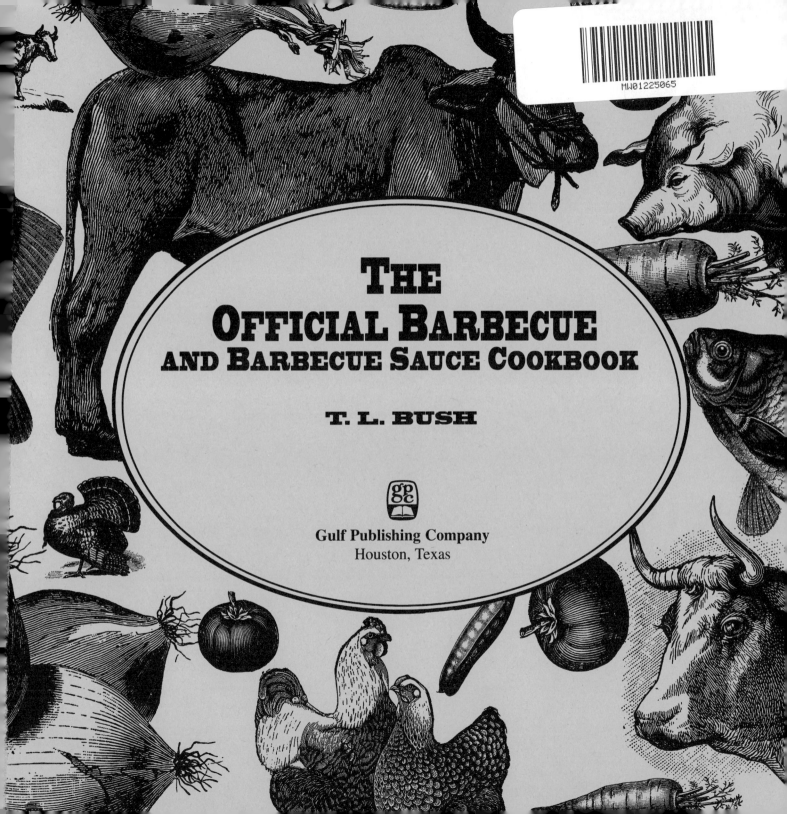

THE
OFFICIAL BARBECUE
AND BARBECUE SAUCE COOKBOOK

T. L. BUSH

Gulf Publishing Company
Houston, Texas

THE OFFICIAL BARBECUE
AND BARBECUE SAUCE COOKBOOK

Gulf Publishing Company
Book Division
P.O. Box 2608 ☐ Houston, Texas 77252-2608

10 9 8 7 6 5 4 3 2 1

Library of Congress Cataloging-in-Publishing Data
Bush, T. L., 1947–
    The official barbecue and barbecue sauce cookbook / T. L. Bush.
      p.   cm.
    Includes index.
    ISBN 0-88415-593-5
    1. Barbecue cookery. I. Title.
TX840.B3B85 1996
641.5′784—dc20   95-45904
                                   CIP

DEDICATION

This book is dedicated to my family and to the many friends and enemies I've gathered along the trails of life. We can't pick our families, but I couldn't have picked a better bunch for mine.

We do get to pick our friends, and I'm proud to say I've picked some good ones. My enemies have sure been good ones as well. I'd say they're some of the best you could find.

To everyone who has been a part of my life, my wish for you is this:

I hope you ride just enough bad horses in your life
to really appreciate the good ones.
And I hope the good ones take you safely down
the trails of life you choose to travel.

CONTENTS

FOREWORD

I know a lady who is a nice, quiet person. She can cook pies, cakes, cookies, and just about any kind of sweets you could desire. When it came to barbecue, she just couldn't get close. To my surprise, she admitted this to me in front of several of our friends. The admission also turned out to be a request for help, thinking I could snap my fingers or wave a magic wand and things would be better. Instead, I asked her a question. I asked, "Do you know how to spell 'tom,' like in tomato?" Her reply, after some strange looks: "Yes, t o m." Then I added, "Do you know how to spell 'pot,' like in potato?" Again, the same puzzled looks, then, "P o t." "Now." I asked, "How do you spell 'timid,' like in barbecue?" All the people in this circle of listeners had a brief little chuckle and most added a comment about my sanity. After repeating the question once more, she finally replied, "There is no timid in barbecue." I just smiled.

Before I get into trouble, let me define the word "pitman."

Pitman: Any being of the human species who can cook over an open pit or cooking device for the purpose of barbecuing.

So from now on if I refer to someone as a pitman, I am not being a sexist and leaving out women.

To be a good pitman, you have to be very confident of your skills. There is no room for timidity. There probably will be several mistakes along the way and you can't let them get to you. Always remember. They were getting ready to throw Columbus overboard because they thought he had made several mistakes.

Ol' fast-on-his-feet Chris calmly looked them in the eyes—all except Pedro, he only had one eye. Chris looked them in the eyes and said, "Get outta' here. We are not lost. I've just been trying to make sure we weren't followed." Well this bought him a couple of days while they all thought about it. Before long their crew again became restless and decided to feed the fishes with Chris. Again they had him at the rail and asked if he had any last requests. "Alas!" He said, "I have but one question. If you do me in, who's going to do the cooking at the big barbecue we got planned when we land?" You see Columbus wasn't a timid person. He knew he could barbecue better than anybody on those boats. They all knew he was an excellent pitman. It is my belief. The strength and courage of a confident pitman saved the life of a great explorer, a great country, and a great little town in Nebraska.

INTRODUCTION

Over the years, I've spent a lot of time traveling to rodeos, cowboy poetry gatherings, chili cook-offs, or whatever. Regardless of the roads I've taken, sooner or later most of them take me by a barbecue joint. The number and names of the places, the pitmen talked to, are long since forgotten. The one thing they all had in common was they were each one different.

I never had much trouble getting the cooks to talk to me about their basic ingredients or cooking times. Many would even tell me some of their little secrets. They just wouldn't tell me how much to use.

As I look back over the notes I've jotted down after leaving these places, I keep coming up with another thing they have in common. None of them give their sauce credit for making their barbecue popular. The one secret ingredient they each shared with me, and didn't know it, was TIME. Every last one of them suggested "time in cooking the meat was the most important thing."

From all the conversations, all the barbecue tasted, and all the miles traveled, there is one thing I know for sure. There are just too many people with too many different tastes for there ever to be the perfect barbecue.

This book is simply a journey into the lives of pitmen and what makes them tick. We will explore the types, cuts, and varieties of meat and fish used. We'll also look at the sauces, rubs, utensils, and the styles of cookers used.

We probably won't solve anything, and more than likely we will arouse the sleeping beast of opinion. All I hope is someone gets a little help in getting started in the barbecue game.

T. L. Bush

THE ORIGIN OF BARBECUE

I don't think any one person, or group of people, can take the credit for originating barbecue. I believe it's a lot like rodeo—it just happened. Nobody can prove they really started it. They woke up one day and there it was.

Like others, I have a theory. We are taught about the caveman and how they probably ate their meals raw. I think one night they left the carcass of a deer hanging in a tree to keep the other critters from eating it. During the night a big storm blew in and lightning struck the tree. The tree caught fire and the deer accidentally got cooked. I can only imagine this did not make these people very happy. Somebody probably caught hell for leaving the deer in the tree instead of putting it away in the cave. If history repeats like they say, it was probably a kid. Well, the ol' man gets mad and tells the kid, "Mooge hugga lakkef smoodda." Which is caveman for, "You left it out, now you eat it." Not wanting to get thumped, he dived in, and much to the surprise of everyone he liked it. He was probably the first "Mikey."

From then on, cavemen kept hanging meat in trees and praying for rain.

Now, I'm sure there were some of my ancestors among these people, and I don't like my meat well done so they probably didn't either. So, obviously being of greater intellect, they started cooking theirs by the heating fire in the cave. I'm sure it was my relatives that had the smarts to take fire inside. If you doubt this scientific made-up fact, I would suggest you ask anybody who knows me or my brothers. I'm sure they will gladly tell you how smart we think we are.

Since that time in history, every race and nationality has tried to lay claim to the origin of barbecue. When, in fact, none of them invented it. They just altered it to fit their tastes.

Before you light the fire, let's look at the choices of what you might cook. Knowing this also will help in the selection of what you are going to cook it on.

I believe anything edible can be cooked for a barbecue. What ever you decide to cook, just make sure it's the best you can get.

Always start by getting the butcher's hidden stock. It's like having a drink of scotch in a bar. Don't settle for what they call "well scotch." Tell that bartender to give you the best he's got. Of all the pitmen I've talked to, quality in meat or fish was stressed.

The choice of cut is up to you. The most common of all meats is beef. Some of the better cuts are:

T-bone, sirloin, porterhouse, tenderloin, and ribeye steaks.

Also good, but a little tougher:

Chuck steak, blade steak, and top-of-the-round steaks.

One of my favorites:

Flank steak, because it cooks faster and when done right is really good.

All of these cuts, if sliced around an inch thick, will cook, over medium to medium-hot heat, in 15 to 40 minutes, Depending on the amount of doneness preferred.

There are more cuts of beef, but I'll touch on them later.

Pork is no doubt the second-most chosen type of meat for barbecues, and there are some great cuts available. Pork chops, sliced ham, and blade steaks are some of the best eatin' this side of heaven.

Some other choices might be:

Lamb chops, bratwurst, smoked sausage, ground meats made into patties, and of course hot dogs.

No, I didn't forget the old standard, ribs. Ribs are a different kind of game and they need a little more preparation than most people think. We'll deal more with ribs later in the cooking section.

Another all-time favorite of the backyard for lunch bunch is chicken. (For those politically correct people, poultry.)

Everything seems to taste like chicken today. I recently gave a four-year-old a bite of an orange. This done only after she looked at me and reminded me it was nice to share. Anyway, I thought it would be humorous to see the pucker of her mouth and the squint in her eyes as she tasted her first slice of real orange. The pucker and squint were there, but so was the comment, "Huh, tastes like chicken."

I don't think anything tastes like chicken but chicken when done right. To me, if something tastes like chicken and it isn't chicken, then somebody goofed when they cooked it.

For best results when barbecuing poultry, again always get the best and freshest you can. I like to use fryers or broilers. They seem to have the best flavor. Old hens or roosters have to much fat and can cause repeated flame-ups. This can cause excessive charring of the outside of the meat and undercooking of the inside. I like my poultry done, not rare.

Along with chicken halyes, breasts, thighs, and drumsticks, you might consider turkey. Turkey cooks in about the same time over medium to medium-hot heat, and has a very good flavor. It tastes like turkey. Cut in breasts, thighs, and legs, it will not remind many people of Thanksgiving.

Some other favorites of mine are: quail, cornish game hen, and pheasant.

When it comes to fish, it's damned hard to beat fresh-caught trout cooked over an open flame in a well-seasoned #10 Griswald. Roll that trout in flour and corn meal, salt and pepper. Gently place it in a shallow bath of hot butter in that skillet and wait for heaven on earth.

You can also barbecue fish if you are careful. I recommend a wire basket with small mesh for cooking fish over hot coals. Always remember to brush oil on the basket mesh before cooking. Fish has a tendency to stick, and it falls apart when you try to remove it.

I have tried to stress the importance of always getting the freshest of anything you are going to barbecue. Well listen up pilgrim, don't fall asleep now. Fresh fish is a must for barbecuing. You don't have to ask anyone about freshness here. Let your nose tell you. Always look for firm flesh, for those of you who might not know, flesh in this case means the meat, not the skin. Make sure the surface is smooth and moist, not slick and slimy. Remember two things: If it smells like chicken, don't buy it; If it has a strong fishy odor, don't buy it. I guess there are really three things. If that is all they have, don't buy it. Buy chicken, slice it thin, and tell everybody it's fish.

Almost everything mentioned so far is best suited for direct heat grilling. That means you can cook it faster and better over direct heat (charcoal, wood coals, or gas heat directly under what you are cooking.) If you are going to cook over a gas flame, avoid any flame-ups, if possible. A big part of barbecuing calls for the outside surface to be cooked to a deep dark crust by the heat involved, not by the burning of a flame. Hot coals from charcoal or wood also can cause flare-ups if the natural juices from what's cooking drips and ignites. So watch for this to happen, because it will. Don't worry if it does; just get a pump bottle of water and put out the flames as they occur.

I mentioned I would touch on other cuts of meat at a later point in time. Well, tick . . . tick . . . it's that time.

For the real barbecue fanatic this is the only true and pure form of barbecue. It involves large portions of meat prepared in a favorite marinate, brushed with magic seasonings, and held in an almost ritualistic manner before being placed on the grill or spit. Something this pure calls for constant attention. Timid pitmen need not apply. As an example, a six-pound boneless rolled rump roast, cooked to a medium doneness, about 160 degrees, will take about two hours cooking time. Figure about 20 minutes a pound over a medium-low heat.

This takes three hours of devotion. At this point you are rereading what you just read. Yes, it only takes two hours to cook it. But, it will require an additional hour to get the heat just right. Then two hours of watching to make sure the heat stays constant and there are no flames to mar the purity of the event.

I am proud to relate the involvement of yours truly at many a gathering. Sizable portions, whole hogs, beef halves, several chickens, turkeys, and burgers have been prepared, and approval was given by those dining on the offerings.

To prepare a half of beef on a turning spit over an open pit does not require meager hours. We're talking days.

The right wood for the base coals. The right meat for the offering, the right rotation speed to cook it properly. The seasonings, the rubs, the sauce.

No, my friends, this ritual is not for the timid, the weak, or the non-dedicated to attempt on his own. But at least once in your life you should try to get in on an event of this size.

Now back to our program. Don't be afraid to attempt cooking a sizable portion of meat. Anything up to six or seven pounds is easy and can be done by anyone with the desire to do it. Just remember 20 minutes per pound of meat over a medium-low heat. Keep the heat constant and wait to enjoy what you have created. I would suggest portions of this size are prepared over indirect heat.

Indirect heat cooking can only be done with a covered grill or pit. The style means just what it says. The meat is placed at one side of the cooking device and the heat source is located at the other. As the covered chamber gets hot, the captured heat and smoke do the cooking.

AM I BARBECUING OR JUST GRILLING AROUND?

To the trained medical practitioner, there are several different technics involved in neurological surgeries. To most of us, it's just brain surgery.

To the purist, to barbecue, one must have the proper equipment. Most times meaning an open pit, a wood-fire base, and hickory chips to add when needed, to maintain purity.

To me, if it walks like a duck, quacks like a duck, and sounds like a duck. It must be a duck. So if you are cooking over an open flame, hot coals, charcoal, direct heat, or indirect heat outdoors and you want to call it barbecuing, you must be barbecuing!

Let's talk about equipment. Most people who enjoy the art of barbecuing dream about their own pit. Complete with rotating spit, firebox, and enough room to cook a cow. When we take a reality check, we find there just isn't room in our second-floor apartments for such pleasure. Do not despair. There is a wide array of good grilling equipment available. The least expensive, if you have a yard, is the simple hole dug in the ground and a grillwork of some kind placed over it. Build your fire on the ground, create a good base of hot coals, put some bricks around the edge of the hole and place your grill on the bricks.

The next step might be the hibachis. These are usually small, portable grills that are made for direct heat-type cooking. Most of them have a grill rack that is adjustable, air vents, and a fire rack that lets ashes fall away.

Next we move to the most common of charcoal grills, the braziers. No, these do not come in cup sizes. This is the uncovered type grill most of us grew up with. Some are made for tabletop use, but most have three legs and a shallow firebox, were designed for charcoal and are made for direct-heat cooking.

I remember my dad getting one of these when we were kids. We thought they just didn't get any better: air vents in the bottom, half a hood to deflect the wind, and a rotisserie.

Most people never used their rotisserie, but my dad did. Like a lot of other folks we couldn't afford the luxury of steaks or chops or anything else fancy, so my dad came up with an idea to feed our family of seven plus our usual playmates and friends: He would buy a big roll of sandwich-size bologna, stick that rotisserie shaft right through the middle and start that baby up. Damn, that was good!

Next we go to the kettle-type grills. These are large kettle-looking things with a domed cover and usually built on three legs. They are designed for direct or indirect heat-type cooking with charcoal or special wood. If a person has limited space, like a second-story balcony in an apartment, these are great. You can cook almost anything with them.

The wagon-style cooker is usually made for charcoal, gas or even electric heat, and can be used for direct or indirect cooking. They have air vents in the bottom, grill hoods to control ventilation, adjustable racks to regulate heat, and are built with two wheels on one set of four legs. The new ones are even available with extra gas burners on each end for cooking other things while you're grilling.

If you're a handy, talented, person and can weld, you can build your own barbecue rig. I've seen hundreds of them across the country. Most of them even work.

When money is not a problem, you can get any kind of rig you want. One with all the bells and whistles, timers, gauges, shelves, smokers, storage areas. You name it, they make it.

For the purist, there is the cinder block pit. If you ever played with Lincoln Logs as a kid, you can build one of these. Start with a hard base, not just dirt. If the ground gets wet, the blocks will sink and create problems. Put down a gravel base if necessary. Start stacking blocks in a rectangle, leaving one end open after the first row of blocks. You will need this space to add firewood or coals. Stack the blocks about four or five high so you don't have to bend over a lot while you are adjusting the meat.

Next you will need some sort of grill to cook on. Something with a mesh design and strong enough to hold the weight of what you are going to cook. Stay away from refrigerator shelves and anything plated with chrome. Once you have found your grillwork, I suggest you build a big fire under it just to start the seasoning process. The only time you will know your grill is seasoned just right is when you have to replace it. True pitmen say there is no such thing as a perfectly seasoned grill. They don't last long enough. I wouldn't worry about this if I were you. First, if you are reading this book, you probably don't know enough about barbecuing to be that far in the game. Second, when you do get that far in, you won't need this book.

Most pitmen keep their heat source of hot coals about six inches thick or their flame low. This way they can cook directly over the heat and not worry about the flames reaching their meat. If your grill is about two to three feet from the fire, you'll be alright.

Now this part might sound strange. Most pitmen I have met prefer to cover the top of the pit and the meat they're cooking with a piece of cardboard box. They want that extra smoke flavor cooked in. Don't worry. If the fire is low, you shouldn't catch the box on fire. So tear a big box apart and try it. That many pitmen can't be wrong.

WHERE THERE'S SMOKE, YOU DON'T WANT FIRE

One of the most important things to remember when barbecuing, is NO FLAMES WHILE YOU ARE COOKING. Unless you are cooking over an open pit where the flames are around two feet away, the flames will cook the meat too fast.

If you have decided to get a grill that recommends charcoal, then there are a few things to know about getting it ready.

1. Never throw the instructions away until after you have it built.
2. After many years of cooking on such a device, I have found if you line the bottom with heavy duty aluminum foil, the unit will last longer.

3. I also like to cover the top of the foil with a two-inch-deep cover of sand.
4. Go back to step number three and be sure to punch out any vent holes you might have in the bottom of your grill.
5. After a few uses, the sand will need to be changed. The reason to have the sand is to catch the grease and other juices that fall from the meat while cooking. This helps keep your grill looking better and helps prevent those unwanted flame-ups.

How Much Wood Would a Woodchuck Chuck?

Well, we don't need to know the answer to that. But we do need to know how much charcoal to use. I have a kind of guideline I go by.

1. Decide what you are going to cook and determine the area it will cover on the grill. Next, cover the bottom of the grill with just enough charcoal to cover same area plus an additional two inches around it.
2. If what you are going to cook is of the size that it will need extended cooking time or it's a windy day, add a little more.

Please remember what I told you earlier. Time is the most important part of barbecuing. Don't get in a hurry starting your fire. Never, never, never use gasoline or kerosene to start your charcoal. The danger aspect should be evident to everyone. But more important to me is the fact that you will ruin the flavor of the meat. The fumes cook right into the meat, and they will stay there.

After you have piled your charcoal in the middle of the firebox, it is customary to squirt some commercial charcoal lighter liquid on them and let them soak it in for about a minute. Then light them with a match. There are also charcoals on the market that already have this starting agent added, but I never could get any of them to work the way they should. All these methods produce a flavor in meat that I don't like.

I have a secret that I use and I hesitate to give it out. My brothers and I market a product that is safer and gives off no odor to ruin the flavor. You can make a similar starter. Get some sawdust and some paraffin. Melt the wax and stir in the sawdust. When this dries it should be crumbly. Place a layer of this under your charcoal and light it. This way you have put no petroleum-based product into your fire, and thus no smell.

There are electric charcoal starters on the market. I don't use one and wouldn't if someone gave me one. I guess they're OK, but they're just not my choice.

I'm always asked about the proper time to start cooking over charcoal. My advice is when your coals have a good glow or they have turned gray with little or no black remaining. A word of caution. Don't walk off and wait for them to turn gray. Check them to be sure they didn't go out.

Another often-asked question is about how to place the hot coals. I like to place mine in one layer and spread them out a little so the drips from what I'm cooking don't cause as many flare-ups. That's for direct-heat cooking.

For indirect-heat cooking. I arrange the hot coals around a drip pan placed in the middle of my cooker under what I'm cooking. This lets the drips fall into the pan and helps keep the grill clean.

How Hot is Cool?

If you are cooking over a gas or electric grill with a heat gauge, your problem is solved. If however you are still of the old set and continue to practice the fine art of fire building, this part might come in handy.

After you have the coals glowing and are ready to start, place your hand, palm down, over your heat source at about the same level your food will be cooking. Start a slow count with each number taking about a second to say. If you have to pull your hand back after a two count your coals are hot. If you can keep it there until three, medium-hot, four, medium, five is the same as a simmer. Six is a low or cool fire. If you are cooking by indirect heat, just remember each count is actually one step lower. Hot coals will provide a medium-hot heat for indirect cooking and so on. I will assume anyone reading this book will know what hot is and that you don't want to touch things that are hot with your bare hands. So I will not bother to advise on cooking utensils. Use what works best for you.

GET READY, GET SET, WAIT!

There are just a few other things to think about before you get started.

1. BEEF doneness. I don't care what anybody tries to tell you. There are only three stages of done for beef.
RARE: Red in the center turning to pink on the edges.
MEDIUM: Just a little pink cast in the center but brown or grayish on the edges.
WELL: Gray throughout with no pink showing.
2. PORK doneness. I prefer to cook pork with no pink or pinkish juices showing. I don't know why. That's just the way I was raised.
3. POULTRY doneness. You don't have to attempt a burnt offering to make sure your poultry is done. Just check the meat next to the bone. If it is not red and juicy, it should be OK.
4. FISH doneness. Fish doesn't take very long to cook, so watch it closely. If the meat is firm and flaky, not soft and mushy, that usually means it's done.
5. VEGETABLE doneness. Any vegetable you might attempt to grill should remain firm, not raw hard, but firm and not mushy.

Now for those of you still lacking the confidence to start living in a world of truly great eating: Please reread this part of the book. For the rest of you, come on, let's eat!

RUB·A·DUB·DUB

This isn't going to be the poetry section. There is a little-known secret among pitmen across the country. Everybody hears barbecue and thinks right away of tomato sauce, vinegar, and sugar. In the southeast, a lot of pitmen use what they call a "rub." A rub is made from dry ingredients. These mixtures are rubbed into the meat before it starts cooking. When you rub it in, it's absorbed into the meat and adds flavors. When you cook it, the rub seals in the natural flavors of the meat as well.

Rubs are made of many different mixtures. In Texas, the most common is a mixture of equal portions of salt, paprika, black pepper, and sugar. A lot of pitmen down here even add a little lemon pepper. You can make your rub from anything you want. Seasoning salt, red pepper, garlic salt, dry mustard, chili powder, and a vast array of other mixtures have been used successfully. I like to make up a bunch of this and have it on hand. It would be stupid of me to try to tell you how much you will need. I don't know how big or what you're cookin'.

Sopping Sauces, Marinades, and Table Sauces

Sops

If you were baking a turkey in your regular oven, sopping would be called basting. But when you are barbecuing, it's called sopping. Sops are applied to the meat at regular intervals. Not too often, though, because every time you open the grill to sop it, you let some of the heat out. You can make a sop out of any ingredients you like. Just remember, don't use sugar or tomato in your sop. These two ingredients cause burning and give the meat a thick coat of sticky yuk.

Don't start sopping until after what you are cooking has reached pit temperature. That way the sop won't run off. If you have a turkey baster, don't use it. A good sop needs to be mopped on with a cotton mop or a brush. You can get these at most notions sections of your grocery store.

My favorite sop takes a full day to make. Time, time, time—the hidden secret of good barbecue.

T.L.'s Private Stock Sop

1 TSP CHILI POWDER	½ CUP CIDER VINEGAR
1 TSP GARLIC SALT	½ CUP WORCESTERSHIRE SAUCE (EASIER
1 TSP TABASCO	PRONOUNCED "WHAT'S THIS HERE SAUCE")
1 TSP PAPRIKA	2 TBSP LEMON JUICE
1 TSP DRY MUSTARD	SALT, PEPPER, AND RED PEPPER TO TASTE
¼ CUP CORN OIL	

Combine everything and let stand in a cool place for at least 24 hours. When all that stuff gets done fighting with each other, it sure makes a good sop.

Make your own sop if you want. You might like it better than mine.

MARINADES

The normal reason to use a marinade is to tenderize and flavor a piece of meat before you cook it. Well, barbecuing makes this unnecessary. The very act of barbecuing will break down the tissue in meat and result in great tenderizing. I don't usually care to use a marinade, but it's OK if you do. I usually want the flavor of the meat to come through, not an artificial flavor. A lot of people like to use a marinade so I'll pass a couple along to you. Again, remember, use whatever you want in your marinades. You're the one doin' the cookin'.

My Part-Time Marinade

2 TBSP GARLIC POWDER	¼ CUP WORCESTERSHIRE SAUCE
⅓ CUP LEMON JUICE	1½ TBSP DRY MUSTARD
⅔ CUP RED WINE	1 TBSP PARSLEY
½ CUP SOY SAUCE	SALT AND PEPPER TO TASTE

This marinade works for beef, poultry, pork, or wild game. Mix everything up in a sizable pan and soak your meat in it for about three hours before cooking. I've even used this as a sop.

I don't remember why I was in Mississippi, but I sure do remember what I did while I was there. This marinade was given to me by someone, I just don't know who. It showed up in my papers several years ago. It seems to me we made up a batch of this stuff. Judging by the ingredients,

I think I know why I don't remember who gave it to me. After all, we only used ¼ cup of the bourbon in the marinade. Anyway, it's good fixin's and I think you might like it.

Dixie Marinade

1½ CUPS WATER	¼ CUP BOURBON
¼ CUP BROWN SUGAR	3 TSP LEMON JUICE
1¼ TSP WORCESTERSHIRE SAUCE	1 4-OZ BOTTLE SOY SAUCE

Mix everything together and pour over meat. Let stand in a cool place for four or five hours. This is best for beef, pork, or wild game. Don't forget that many of the marinades can be used for sops as well.

Any marinade you find in any other cookbook will work. So if you're partial to marinades, have at it.

TABLE SAUCES

When we mention barbecue sauces, most people actually think of table sauces: Sauces you would use to flavor the meat just before you eat it. There are a lot of prepared table sauces on the market, and some of them are even good.

Really, there are the three types of sauces. We have just described two of them. Marinades to flavor and tenderize the meat before cooking, sops to flavor and tenderize the meat during cooking, and the third one is the table sauces. This one will usually make or break a good barbecue.

As you travel the country, you will find a wide variety of sauces. Most of the Texas sauces are thick, tomato-based sauces.

Move on east, and the sauces are still sweet. They use more sugar, syrup, honey, and brown sugar. I think the mixtures tend to compliment the flavor of pork, which they cook a lot more. These ingredients are usually added to a ketchup-mustard base. Keep in mind, ketchup is usually 57% sugar.

Get into the Carolinas and it's a different ball game. North Carolina tends to favor tomato-based sauces, while South Carolina leans more to the mustard-based sauce—except for northeast North Carolina, which prefers a vinegar-based sauce.

I'm sure there are those of you wondering why I failed to include Tennessee in one of these listings. Well, I had the pleasure of living in Tennessee for awhile, and I'm not really sure what style they prefer. In my quest of barbecue, I found everything imaginable. That state has had so many folks come through it, on their way south and west, from so many different places, I think they can do it all.

Head north and along the east coast, and you will find they seem to prefer the vinegar-based barbecue sauces. This choice came with the people who settled that region. If there was a first barbecue sauce for this country, I think it would be a toss-up between the European settlers of the northeast and the Spanish settlers of southwest Texas.

I hope you can see now why I don't believe there is such a thing as the perfect barbecue sauce. There are to many different tastes in this country for one sauce to please everybody.

I will just give you a sampling of various sauces from across the country so you can create a starting point for yours. Sauces are like rubs, sops, and marinades: They should express your tastes. So find a base sauce you like, and add or subtract what you want to reach the flavor you desire.

I think it's only fitting and proper to start with my favorite kind of sauces, the ones from the big "T." You guessed it. I'm talkin' Texas.

Texas Table Sauce

1 STICK MARGARINE (8 TBSP)   ⅓ CUP LEMON JUICE
⅓ CUP KETCHUP   ⅓ CUP VINEGAR
⅓ CUP WORCESTERSHIRE SAUCE   1 TBSP TABASCO
SALT AND PEPPER TO TASTE

Melt margarine in saucepan. Add liquids and bring to boil. Add dry seasonings. Let stand refrigerated for 3 or 4 days. Use this as a table sauce or sop it on during the last 20 minutes of cooking.

Big "T" Table Sauce

⅓ CUP VEGETABLE OIL   3 CUPS KETCHUP
1 CUP WORCESTERSHIRE   ½ CUP BROWN SUGAR
½ CUP CHOPPED ONIONS   ⅔ CUP LEMON JUICE
½ CUP WATER   3 DASHES RED PEPPER
1 DASH PAPRIKA   DASH SALT, PEPPER

Heat oil in sauce pan. Add all the ingredients. Cover and let cook over low heat for about an hour or until thick.

This is a sauce I picked up in Tennessee. Strangely enough, when you're in a hurry, which I don't recommend, it's not bad.

Soda Pop Sauce

1 CAN SODA POP (ANY KIND AS LONG AS IT HAS COLOR)
½ CUP BROWN SUGAR   1 CUP KETCHUP

Mix it all in a sauce pan. Bring to boil. Reduce heat and let simmer about a half hour.

On one of my many travels across this great country of ours, I happened to stop at an out-of-the-way truck stop. This was back when you could count on truck stop food being good, homemade, and fresh, not frozen. Anyway, it was about three in the morning and I had just finished a long drive.

As a rule, back then you could ask for a daily special and they had something worth eating. So I asked and was told the special of the day was "MULE'S FOOT BARBECUE." Naturally I asked about the name and was told it had a lot of kick.

When I travel I always like to sample one of three things: biscuits and gravy, fried chicken, or barbecue. The name sold me, so I went with the "MULE'S FOOT."

I didn't know if I was just tired enough or if it really was good. So I asked the waitress what was in it. She knew all the ingredients but she just didn't know how much of each. When I asked if I could talk to the cook, she allowed as how she didn't think that would be a good idea. I have learned a few things in this life, some of which are: You could usually trust a truck stop waitress, especially if she was old enough to be your mother; and don't get anybody mad at you at three in the morning when you're just passin' through.

After some trial and error this is the list I came up with for old "MULE'S FOOT."

Mule's Foot

1 CUP KETCHUP	1½ CUP REAL STRONG BLACK COFFEE
⅓ CUP LEMON JUICE	1 STICK MARGARINE
1⅓ CUP WORCESTERSHIRE SAUCE	1½ TSP SUGAR
2 TSP RED PEPPER	1 DASH SALT

Mix it all in a sauce pan and simmer for about 45 minutes.

Everybody needs to start somewhere, so this is a basic sauce I think is used all over the country. This is a good one to make those changes to until you find the flavor you want.

Your Basic Starter Sauce

1 CUP KETCHUP	2 DASHES HOT SAUCE
1 TSP MINCED ONION	½ CUP WATER
2 TSP BROWN SUGAR	⅓ CUP VINEGAR
1 TSP WORCESTERSHIRE SAUCE	1 PINCH OF SALT

Put everything into a pan and bring to a boil. Turn it down and let it simmer for about 20 minutes. This is a nice gentle sauce that shouldn't offend anyone. It has just enough twang to it to be called barbecue sauce.

If your tastes happen to go for the tangy twang to your sauce, then try this one. I picked this one up in the hills of east Tennessee. I've got family there and they sure know how to cook.

Townsend Twang Sauce

⅓ CUP VINEGAR	⅓ CUP WHITE SYRUP
¼ CUP CHOPPED ONION	1 CUP KETCHUP
1 TSP LEMON JUICE	1 PINCH OF SALT
HOT SAUCE TO TASTE	

Like everything else, mix it all in a pan and bring it to a boil. Reduce heat to a simmer and let cook about 15 minutes.

Most people have had the opportunity to try a sampling of Buffalo Wings—named for a location in New York, not the mammal. These rascals kind of grow on you. If you want to impress your friends and make them think you know something, try this. Wings won't take long to cook over a medium-hot indirect heat. When they are just about done, start sopping them with this little mixture. I got this from a pitman in upstate New York and it came with this warning.

WARNING: This sauce is not to be consumed by those of weak nature or gentle mouth, members of the clergy, and others with strong religious connections. If you liked the "Beast" better as a man, thought "Bambi" was too scary for children, or cried when they shot "Ol' Yeller," you may not be tough enough for this sauce.

Ring-O-Fire Sauce

1 MEDIUM ONION	1 BIG CLOVE GARLIC
2 TBSP CORN OIL	⅓ CUP MOLASSES
½ CUP VINEGAR	1 TSP SALT
1⅔ CUP KETCHUP	1 TBSP CAYENNE
1½ TBSP TABASCO SAUCE	1 TSP DRY MUSTARD
1 TBLSP CHILI POWDER	

Chop the onion, press and mince the garlic, add the oil, and cook in saucepan until onion is tender. For this next part I suggest you go to your music collection and dig out an old Eagles album, tape or CD. Find the 1976 version of LIFE IN THE FAST LANE by Henley, Frey, and Walsh.

This is the particular song we were listening to when he first made this for me. For some reason it seems to make it work better.

After you have the onions and garlic cooked down, add everything else and bring it to a boil. Reduce the heat and let it cook uncovered on low for about 30 minutes. There should be enough of this batch that you can put the unused portion in a GLASS jar. Do not use metal or plastic.

So now you are ready for those tough, fire eating, friends of yours. I think another warning should be added. Do not kiss anyone after eating this sauce. It has a peculiar way of hanging around.

I am proud to say I have family in the hills of east Tennessee. I am also very proud to call them my friends. For most cases they are normal, quiet, productive, friendly, and well-off. However, there are a couple that tend to make a feller wonder. While they appear normal on the outside, they have peculiar ways about them.

While visiting one summer, one of my cousins asked if I would like to come over the next morning. He was going to start some barbecue sauce and thought I might like to help. Being naturally nosy, I jumped at the chance.

I thought his request for my being there at five a.m. was a little strange, but what the heck. They do things a little different down there.

Five a.m. came and I was there and so was he. I got out of my truck only to be told to get into his. I watched as he loaded two of his dogs in the back and then climbed behind the wheel.

The old truck blew blue smoke as he cranked it over, and on the second try it fired right off. A smile came across his face and then the words, "We're off." I smiled, but deep down inside I was trying to figure out why we were in his truck with two dogs, driving down an old logging road going to make barbecue sauce.

Nothing was said for a while, then he looked over, and said, "Don't try to pet my dogs." I said, "What?" He said, "Don't try to pet my dogs. They don't take well to strangers." I assured him I would respect his request. In my mind I was wondering why anyone would offer their hand to a snarling pit bull.

After another 20 minutes I could take no more. "Where in the hell are we goin'?" I asked. He looked at me like I was the only one lost and said, "To make barbecue sauce like I said last night." I calmly asked, "Why do we need dogs to make barbecue sauce?"

"I'll show ya'," he said. We stopped a few minutes later and he turned the dogs loose. Off through the woods they went. Before long they hit a trail and the noise got louder. Just as I guessed, off we went right behind 'em. About an hour later, we got within sight of 'em. I could tell there was a fight of some kind going on but not 'til I got closer could I see they were fighting a big old black bear. My heart didn't just skip a beat. It was halfway back to the truck without me.

"No matter what happens, don't try to pet my dogs," echoed in my mind. What a joke! We stopped about 30 yards from the disagreement and watched. Nobody was getting hurt and nobody was winning. Finally the bear sent one of the dogs flyin' through the air. Then he bolted and ran off through the woods. The dogs gave chase for a while, then came back to where we were.

"What in the hell does any of this have to do with making barbecue sauce?" I asked. "Honey," was his reply. I looked him in the eyes and said, "Dogs or no dogs. Don't you go funny on me now."

He turned and pointed. Right where the fight was goin' on was a hollowed-out tree. As I looked up the tree, I saw one of the most fearful sights I've ever seen. A massive swarm of bees. "Holy Crap," I whispered. "We gotta' get out of here." "After we smoke them bees and get some of that fresh honey." he laughed. "Smoke them bees Hell!" I yelled. "I'm allergic to bee stings!" He looked at me and calmly said, "Well, just be careful and don't get stung. 'Cause I ain't carrying you outta' here."

After all that, this is the recipe he shared with me. No, let me state that differently. This is the recipe I earned.

Fightin' Good Honey Sauce

1 MEDIUM ONION	⅓ CUP HONEY (I SUGGEST
2 TBSP CORN OIL	YOU BUY IT)
2 TBSP CHILI POWDER	1 CLOVE GARLIC
2 TBSP WORCESTERSHIRE SAUCE	1 CUP TOMATO SAUCE
2 TBSP YELLOW MUSTARD	2 SHOTS SOUR MASH

Cook the onion and garlic in the oil until the onion is tender. Add rest of ingredients and bring to a boil. Reduce the heat to a simmer and let cook uncovered about 30 minutes. Even if you don't favor the sweet-style sauces, you really ought to try this just for the hell of it. It's actually good.

My life has been blessed and cursed like many others, but I can't complain. The good Lord has been mighty tolerant of my actions and has seen fit to let me have many great adventures.

One of the truly great adventures in my life was owning John Waynes' movie horse "Dollor." I traveled all over the country with that horse and met a lot of nice people. "Dollor" was a fine animal and a good friend.

On one of my trips to California, I stopped off in a little out-of-the-way place for lunch. Naturally I ordered barbecue, and this is the way the sauce was prepared.

California Hot Barbecue Sauce

4 CLOVES GARLIC, MASHED AND CHOPPED

1 DASH SALT

1 SMALL ONION

1 TBSP CHILI POWDER

½ CUP VINEGAR

1 CUP OLIVE OIL

1 SMALL GREEN PEPPER

1 CUP TOMATO SAUCE

1 TSP OREGANO

Chop the garlic, onion, and green pepper. Combine with all the other ingredients and simmer for 20 minutes. I still haven't figured out why the lady called this a hot sauce, but that's what she called it. I've tried it with different additions and it's about the same. Some things I have added are: Tabasco, Worcestershire, red pepper, mustard, and even sugar.

This is another California sauce that I was given for my collection. The folks told me this was an old recipe that had been handed down for years. It's not hot in any way. There's not even any pepper in it. I think it's just different enough to be good.

Smooth Sauce

3 CLOVES GARLIC	½ CUP VINEGAR
1 CUP WATER	1 TSP SALT
1 TBSP MINCED ROSEMARY	½ CUP CORN OIL
¼ CUP MINCED MINT LEAF	¼ CUP CHOPPED ONION

Cook all the ingredients together at a simmer for 20 minutes. Strain before using.

While we are on the subject of Californians and their sauces, I think it's time to relate a little history about its people.

The West Coast has a history of great length. When the first Spanish Dons came to the region, they brought with them the art of barbecuing. They had massive fiestas and fed hundreds of people.

As the West developed and more people moved in, barbecue remained very popular and to this day it is almost a ritual. Although today's barbecuing is done on a lesser scale, they have had some really big feeds.

One such feed allegedly involved over sixty thousand people, twelve tons of beef, thousands of pounds of red beans, and a 100 pounds of chili powder.

The story goes that they dug several huge pits and lined them with rocks. Fires were built in the pits and allowed to burn for half a day. This produced a deep bed of hot coals. They then placed a huge sheet of iron on the tops of these pits and several layers of wet burlap sacks. After that they placed the meat, cut into 25-pound chunks wrapped in cheesecloth and soaked in sauces, on top. They covered this with more sacks and boards and then covered the whole thing with sand to keep in the heat. They let this cook about 14 hours and it is said to have turned out quite tender. Now that was a barbecue.

There are so many different sauces that have been given to me that I will never live long enough to try them all. I do pledge, however, to at least try.

I found these next two sauces written on napkins folded inside some books that had been packed away for some time. I don't know where they came from, and I had never tried them. After reading them, I said to myself, "Self, you're writing a barbecue book. This might be a good time to try 'em." So I did.

I was getting ready to barbecue a green ham that weighed about 5 pounds and decided to try this one.

From the Valley of the Lost Sauce

4 TBSP CHOPPED ONION	½ TSP CHILI POWDER
½ TSP PEPPER	¼ TSP CINNAMON
1 TSP SALT	1 TSP PAPRIKA
½ TSP DRY MUSTARD	1 CLOVE GARLIC PRESSED
2 TBSP WORCESTERSHIRE	3 TBSP VINEGAR
1 10 OZ CAN TOMATO SAUCE	½ CAN (5 OZ) WATER

Mix all these things together and simmer for about 30 minutes. I then sliced the ham and placed it in a pan and poured this sauce over it. Then I put it back on the fire and let it cook on a medium-hot heat for another 30 minutes. It was good.

From the Valley of the Lost Sauce II

2 TBSP WORCESTERSHIRE	1 TBSP SALT
½ TSP RED PEPPER	½ TSP BLACK PEPPER
1 TSP PAPRIKA	1 TBSP CHILI POWDER
¼ TSP ALLSPICE	2 TBSP MINCED ONION

Mix everything in a pan and cook over medium heat for about 45 minutes. Use as a sop for the last 30 minutes of cooking for your ribs. It also makes a good table sauce.

This is another lost-and-found sauce. I tried it on a batch of ribs. I think you might like it also.

I have attempted to give to you a sampling of table sauces for reference. Now is the time for you to decide what your choice of the day may be. As you get deeper into the barbecue world you will find that different cuts of meat may dictate what sauce you would prefer.

The sauces offered will act as a good guideline for the creation of your own. It might be that you are not that fond of what is offered. If this is so, then you might want to purchase a commercial sauce and work with it. I'll bet you can find a mixture that pleases your palate.

RIBS . . .
RIBS . . .
RIBS . . .

Ever since the creation of this world and the inclusion of mankind, ribs have been a controversial subject. If the story of Eve had been told using a toe bone instead of a rib, maybe we wouldn't be so fussy about ribs.

There seems to be more rib recipes then any others for barbecuing. I find this rather strange. Why take something so good and so easy to fix and complicate it?

Yes, the preparation of ribs can be shortened. For those of you who wish to do so, this a common method. Whatever type ribs you are going to grill should be cut in serving-size portions and boiled until they are just about done, then placed on the grill and some kind of sauce brushed on for the remaining cooking time. I don't care for this method, but if you do that's fine.

I refuse to let time dictate my barbecuing methods. I have related elsewhere that almost all the great pitmen have indicated TIME is of utmost importance. Ribs are a shining example of what can happen if you take the time to do it. The parboiling of ribs might get them to the table faster, but what do you lose when you drain them? Flavor and natural juices are poured down the drain.

I prefer, instead, to let the very act of barbecuing do the tenderizing of the ribs I cook. I realize not everybody has a covered grill and the boiling method might work best for them so they don't overcook the ribs because of the direct heat. But, in my humble opinion, the best ribs are done over indirect heat and done slowly.

There are three kinds of ribs: loin ribs (also called baby back ribs when cut from a young hog), back ribs, and spareribs. All three are great for barbecuing. If you are trying to impress your guests, use the loin ribs, they cost more but they have the most meat.

Before you start cooking ribs, always make sure they have been skinned. There is a thin membrane covering the bone side of the ribs. This membrane should be skinned off. If it hasn't, you can do it with a sharp knife.

Some people like to cut the ribs into serving portions before they cook 'em. You guessed it, I don't. If the ribs are too large for you to handle on your grill, just cut them into portions you can. I think cutting them smaller makes them cook too fast and tends to make them dry.

Now, take your ribs and using a dry rub of your choice, rub it into both sides of the ribs. Rub it into the meat, not just on it. Let them stand until they come to room temperature while you start the fire. When the fire is medium, this will mean the cooking side is medium-low. Place the ribs over a drip pan, bone side down, away from the coals or gas heat.

Cooking time will vary depending on the size slab of ribs you are doing and the number of times you open the grill. Most pitmen use a rule of thumb of an hour a pound. When the outside meat starts to feather, or separate, the ribs are probably done.

Since you have used a rub, you might not want to use too much sauce while cooking. Sopping a couple of times late into the process won't hurt, but remember, every time you open that grill you lose heat. I suggest waiting until the last 15 minutes or so to sop.

If you are serving several guests, I would suggest offering three types of table sauce. This is the best method I have found to please most everyone. A mild basic sauce, a twangy sauce, and a hot sauce should cover all the bases and make everybody happy.

To become a good pitman, it is your job to cook the meat just right. Let everyone else choose their own type of sauce. If the meat is done right and they are happy with their choice of sauce, they will leave your feed thinking how great a pitman you are.

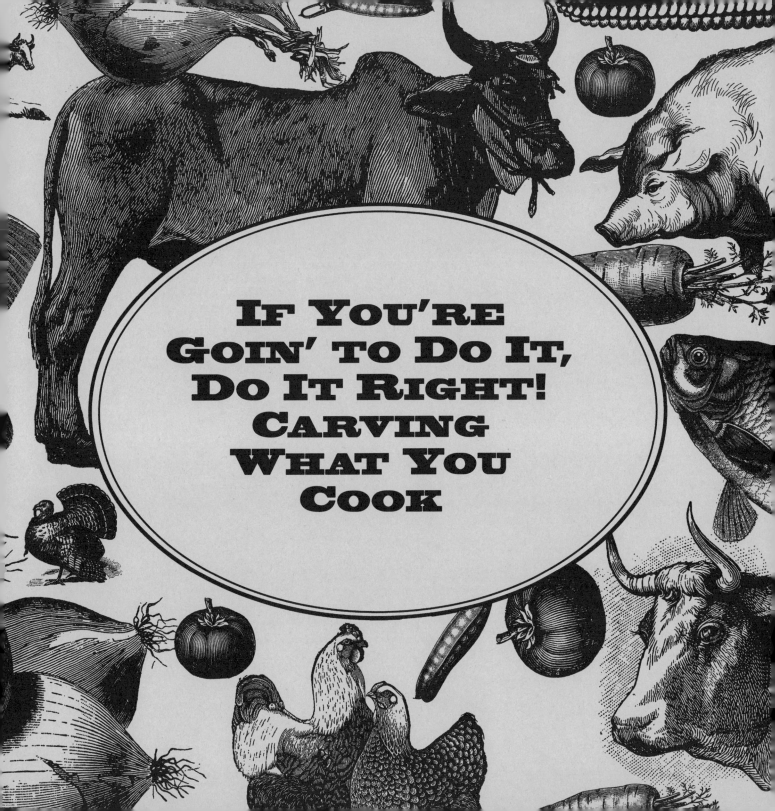

If You're Goin' to Do It, Do It Right! Carving What You Cook

Sometimes I forget there are readers who are just starting to cook. I guess I've been cooking for so long I assume everyone knows how.

When I was growing up—there are those who wonder when I will finish this effort—I was number four of five boys, and the need to learn to cook was a matter of self-preservation. My father worked three jobs and sometimes my mother worked two. Unlike many people today who look back and blame their parents for their problems, we had the best parents and upbringing you could want. I never realized how poor we were until I was out on my own. My mother could manage to cook enough to feed all of us and many of our unexpected friends. She was magic in the kitchen. She taught all of us the basics in cooking, cleaning, sewing, laundry, and manners. Our father always seemed to be working, but he always was there when we needed him.

Along with the basic skills of boyhood to manhood, his gift to us in life was to teach us right from wrong. In today's politically correct world, his methods and reasoning would be quite difficult to comprehend. They would face much difficulty in application. There would be a need for support groups, civil liberties legal eagles, university studies, and probably several television shows to disclose the hidden agenda of his theory. I will attempt to pass this difficult method of educating children to those of you that are interested. YES meant yes and NO meant no! There was no gray area. No my father was not abusive, but if he said it, he meant it, and we knew to take heed. We also learned his hand didn't fit in our back pocket.

You may be asking what any of this has to do with barbecuing? I think their guidance and interest in our lives made us better, more confident adults. This confidence is passed on in everything, even our cooking.

As an illustration of their guidance, they even impressed upon us the importance of properly carving what we cooked. It was stressed that cooking something right was primary. But, this effort could be for nothing if you carved the meat, fish, or poultry wrong.

As I related at the beginning of this tangent. I realize there are those of you who are new to this cooking game. So I will try to explain the best way to carve and serve what you have cooked.

I would first suggest getting to know where what you are cooking came from. Knowing this will allow you to determine what bone or joints you will encounter. This doesn't need to be a college short course. Once you have looked at this, your carving will be much easier.

Most steaks, chops, or chicken pieces will be carved by those being served. I would suggest you remove any excess fat or bone from these pieces. This will allow your guests to be more at ease and less likely to be embarrassed by an accident while trying to cut their meat. We wouldn't want Aunt Claire to smack Uncle Charlie with a flying piece of meat.

For those big chunks of meat, always remember to carve across the grain of the meat. The thickness of the slices will vary with the type of cut you are serving, and may be influenced by the personal preference of those for whom the carving is being done. Generally the slices should be thin, but regardless of thick or thin they should be neat and even.

TENDERLOIN—Hold the loin firmly with a fork and cut the meat squarely the grain in slices about one-half inch thick. Always begin with the thick portion. This is done for a couple of reasons. First it will allow you to get more even slices from the larger end. Second, it will allow you to have something to eat while everyone else is served. I call those small, end pieces my private stock. I think they're too good for anybody else.

ROUND or RUMP ROAST—Cut across the grain, but carve the slices as thin as possible. This is done because these cuts of meat are less tender than others.

STANDING RIB ROAST—If it is a good-sized roast, the best way to carve it is to stand it upright. Upright means with the ends of the ribs and the section of the backbone resting on the cutting board. This will place the fat layer on top. Below this fat layer is a layer of not-so-tender meat, but below that is the tender heart of the roast.

Stick a fork firmly into the top of the roast at the thin end. Starting at the thick end, slice the roast in thin slices. Slice through the layer of fat, the not-so-tender meat and the heart of the roast until the knife hits the bone. After you have sliced several slices in this manner, turn the knife and take the tip and cut the meat away from the bone. (WARNING: Have your table sauce ready, this stuff will disappear in a hurry.)

ROLLED ROAST—A rolled roast should be held together with skewers. Set the roast on end and stick a fork into the side an inch or two from the top. Holding the knife horizontally, slice the meat in thin, even slices across the entire surface of the roast. Remove the skewers as you reach them and move the fork downward as needed.

HAM—This will depend on how you are serving it. If served as steaks, slice it across the grain in pieces about one-half inch thick. If for sandwiches, slice it thin. In any case, I like to remove any fat so my guests are not bothered by it. If the ham still has the bone in, slice several pieces down to the bone, then turn your knife and slice them free from the bone.

I am, by nature, a cheapskate. I see no reason to pay someone to cut up a chicken when I can do it for free. This way I also get it cut the way I want it. As a rule, I like to barbecue chicken halves instead of pieces. Most people are not like this and prefer to do pieces because they feel they can get it done better and one bird will serve more than two people. Whatever your choice, I will attempt to describe the way I cut up a chicken.

After you have cleaned the bird—even birds bought in groceries need cleaning—and removed all the pin feathers, quill stubs etc., sit the bird up with the back toward you. Insert the knife tip into the hole at the top where the neck used to be. Staying to the right of the back bone, cut from top to bottom. This will divide the bird at the back. Now open the bird so you can see the back of the breast bone. Lay the bird flat with the exposed insides up. Place the tip of your knife in the middle of the breast bone and push down. This will crack the breast bone and allow you to cut through the breast and finish separating the halves. With the bird now halved, take each half and place it skin side up. Turn the half so the back is away from you. As you look at the bird there is an imaginary line that runs from top to bottom at an angle that separates the breast from the thigh and leg. Turn your knife so it is above this line and place the thick part of the knife across the back bone. Put pressure on the knife and cut through the backbone and draw the blade downward through the skin. This will quarter the bird.

Holding the breast with one hand, lift the wing up until you see where the joint is that holds it to the breast. Cut through this joint to separate the two. Cut through the leg and thigh joint and where the thigh joins the back. You have now cut up a chicken and saved a few cents. Don't worry if you don't get it right the first time. Practice will improve your skills.

POULTRY—Whole turkey or chicken. Let the bird rest on its back on a cutting board. Turn the legs so they are pointing to your left. Insert a fork into the drumstick and cut around the hip joint. Apply downward pressure with the fork to expose the hip joint, then cut through the hip joint with your knife. This will allow the leg to be easily removed. Leave the fork in the drumstick and place it flat on the cutting board, then cut the meat away from the thigh and remove it to a platter. The drumstick is usually not offered to the guests unless someone wants it.

Next, place your fork low in the side of the bird. Slice the breast downward in thin, even slices. Remove this to the other platter. Do the same thing to the other side and you've got it made.

Do the same thing with domestic ducks, but remember wing joints are farther toward the back than in chicken or turkeys. If you grill wild ducks, only the breast is usually served.

Although I am a strong advocate of catch and release, I still keep a few fish for my other belief: Catch and eat. Pan-size trout, bass, or panfish can be served as cooked to your guests, and they can figure out how they want to eat it.

If you do not have a set of knives for carving fish, a table knife should do. In serving carved fish to your guests, it is important to try to serve as little bone as possible. In serving thick pieces or middle cuts of fish like salmon or cod, place the section skin up. Carve the fish in thick slices down to the bone, then slip the knife under the portions and remove them from the bone.

I hope this will help those of you that didn't know and will serve as a reminder for those that did. It doesn't really matter how you serve it as much as how you carve it. If carved properly, the natural tenderness of barbecuing will only be improved. Get the table sauce ready and enjoy.

Man Does not Live by Barbecue Alone

A good barbecue should center on the meat being offered, but the side dishes will make them even better. Like any meal you might prepare, the choice of the menu is yours. There are, however, a few old standbys that are a sure thing when it comes to pleasing your guests. Here are a few that are easy to make and good, too.

(HINT: If you are taking the time to have a real barbecue, take the time to fix fresh side dishes. Use the freshest vegetables you can get, and don't rush the preparation.)

T.L.'s Baked Beans

2 CUPS PEA BEANS	½ TSP SALT
1 SMALL ONION (SLICED)	½ TSP DRY MUSTARD
4 STRIPS SMOKED BACON	2 TBSP MOLASSES

Soak beans in cold water overnight. (HINT: To take some of the gas out of beans, add a tablespoon of baking soda to the water.) When you are ready to start cooking, pour off the soak water and cover with fresh. Simmer until the skins start to crack, drain water, and pour beans into covered bean pot, over onion. Push bacon strips into beans, leaving very little exposed. Mix salt, dry mustard, and molasses in a cup, fill with hot water, stir until well-mixed, and pour over beans. Add enough water to cover and bake at 300 degrees for 6 to 7 hours. Check from time to time and add enough water to cover until the last hour. Remove the cover and bring bacon strips to the top so they can brown.

Carrots don't have to be sliced and mixed with other things to be served. I'm not usually much on carrots, but this is one way I like them.

Crunch Carrots

There really is no list of ingredients for this, because it will depend on how many carrots you want to fix.

Wash and scrape the carrots. If you are using young carrots leave them whole. If you are going to use old carrots, slice them lengthwise. Boil them about 15–20 minutes or until tender, in water containing 1 teaspoon of sugar. Just before they are done cooking, salt the water. When done, drain, roll in butter and then in crushed corn flakes, and brown in oven at 350 degrees.

This colorful little dish helps add to the festivities at a good backyard cookout.

T.L 's Red and Yellow Stuff

2 CUPS COOKED CORN	1 TSP SUGAR
2 CUPS TOMATOES	1 CUP BREAD CRUMBS
1 TSP SALT	PEPPER TO TASTE

Mix all the seasonings with corn and tomatoes, and pour into a greased baking dish. Sprinkle the bread crumbs over the top and bake at 350 degrees for 30 minutes. (HINT: This works well in using up leftover corn or tomatoes.)

This green bean salad is a little different from what you might be used to, but it sure is good.

Dressed Green Bean Salad

2 CUPS COOKED GREEN BEANS

1 TBSP MINCED ONION

½ CUP FRENCH DRESSING

1 HARD BOILED

EGG YOLK

Soak green beans and onion in dressing for at least one hour. Drain and place beans and onion in serving dish. Sprinkle crumbled egg yolk over the top. (HINT: This also works for leftover beans.)

Now, I'm your plain-old everyday kind of guy who likes slaw just as much, if not more than others. But on one of my trips to California, I happened to stop at a barbecue joint in the northern part. As I sat there, looking out over a lake, the owner came up to take my order. I don't remember what I ordered, but with it I ordered slaw. He asked if I wanted good slaw or the usual. Not wanting to get sick, 3,000 miles from home, I asked what he meant. "Well, there's the usual kind of slaw everybody from back east eats. And then there's my own slaw," he said. Being reasonably sure I wasn't going to get something bad, I ordered his special. Damn it was good. I commented on the greatness of his mixture and started in on the con to acquire the recipe. I wasn't having much luck until he asked what I was doing out there. I informed him I was the proud owner of John

Wayne's movie horse Dollor and that I was on tour with him. As I watched his eyes widen and a smile come to his face, I knew I was going to get that recipe. His only request was to pet Dollor, but I worked my trade, got the recipe, and he got to ride the horse that carried a legend. In honor of the horse, I named this slaw in his name.

Lucky Dollor Slaw

1 SMALL HEAD CABBAGE	1 TSP DRY MUSTARD
2 APPLES, CHOPPED	1 TBSP SUGAR
1 MEDIUM ONION, MINCED	1 TBSP MELTED BUTTER
2 MINCED PIMIENTOS	⅓ CUP LEMON JUICE
3 HARD BOILED EGGS	½ CUP WHIPPED CREAM
¼ TSP SALT	PARSLEY

Shred cabbage and mix it with apples, onion, and pimientos. Rub yolks of eggs to a paste and add salt, sugar, mustard, and butter. Mix thoroughly until smooth. Stir in lemon juice and mix. Add the whipped cream and mix it all with the cabbage mixture. Garnish with egg whites from the boiled eggs. Sprinkle with parsley. This batch will serve about six, so add accordingly for more guests.

There are almost as many recipes for potato salad as there are barbecue sauces. There are ethnic styles, hot styles, sweet, sour, cold, and on and on. I found this one in Idaho, strangely enough, and I like it. I thought maybe you would, too.

Potato Salad

1 QUART POTATOES
1 TBSP CORN OIL
2 TBSP VINEGAR
1 ONION

1 TBSP CHOPPED PARSLEY
SALT AND PEPPER
MAYONNAISE
2 STALKS CELERY

Boil potatoes with skin on and let them cool before peeling. Leaving the skin on during cooking keeps the potato firm and not mushy. Firm potatoes make better salad. After they are peeled, cut into small pieces and add oil and vinegar. Chop onion and celery fine, add parsley, then salt and pepper to taste. Add enough mayonnaise to give the potatoes a thin coat, then mix. I like to sprinkle a little paprika on top for color. Sliced boiled eggs also look nice.

These are just a few basic side dishes that are always in good taste at a backyard barbecue. Just remember, "It's your party, serve whatever you want." Cook with confidence and pleasure. If it looks good, smells good, and tastes good, you've done it right.

WHEN DO WE EAT?

I have tried to give a basic idea on how you can tell when what you are cooking is done. To simplify this I hope this approximated cooking time guide will help.

Remember, direct grilling is having what you are cooking directly over the heat source. Refer to the "How Hot Is Cool" section for cooking temps.

Grill the meat, uncovered for the approximate times listed, turning the meat over once about halfway through the cooking time.

CUT THICKNESS	DONENESS	TIME	HEAT
BEEF			
Steak			
T-bone, porterhouse, ribeye, and sirloin			
½ inch	Rare	15 to 20 min	Med-Hot
	Medium	20 to 25 min	Med-Hot
	Well	25 to 30 min	Med-Hot
Round, chuck, and blade			
1 inch	Rare	15 to 20 min	Medium
	Medium	20 to 25 min	Medium
	Well	25 to 30 min	Medium

For each additional ½ inch of thickness of the cut, add an additional 5 min. of cooking time.

Flank steak			
¾ inch	Medium	15 min	Medium

(continued on next page)

53

CUT	THICKNESS	DONENESS	TIME	HEAT
VEAL CHOP				
	¾ inch	Well	10+ min	Med–Hot
LAMB CHOP				
	1 inch	Rare	10 to 15 min	Medium
		Med	15 to 20 min	Medium
		Well	20 to 25 min	Medium
PORK				
Blade steak				
	½ inch	Well	10+ min	Med–Hot
Ham slices				
	1 inch	Well	20+ min	Med–Hot
Chops				
	¾ inch	Well	10 to 12 min	Med–Hot
	1½ inch	Well	30 to 40 min	Medium

DIRECT-GRILLING POULTRY

Today's politically correct statement in cooking is to remove the skin from poultry before cooking. This is to show you are a better person and care more than those who don't do it. I am not of this school of thought. There is a lot of good flavor in that skin, and eating some of it from time to time won't hurt most people. I do not propose a daily diet of high fat, and due to health reasons, even I watch my fat intake.

Your diet is just like your habits. If you eat the things that are good for you, and not a lot of junk foods, your health will be easier to maintain. If your habits are those that are clean, good, and don't bring harm to others, you should have a happy life.

Another reason I like to grill with the skin on is to help keep in the flavors, and keep the meat moist. The skin also acts as a good wick for the addition of sauces. It holds the blends of spices and herbs mixed in the sauce close to the meat and allows it to be absorbed.

BIRD	SIZE	TIME	HEAT TEMP.
CHICKEN			
Fryer halves	1½ lbs	40 to 50 min	Medium
Chicken breasts, thighs, drumsticks	2, 2½ lbs	35 to 45 min	Medium
Breasts, boned	5 oz	15 min	Med–Hot
Cornish hens	4 lb	45 min	Med–Hot
TURKEY			
Breasts	8 oz	15 min	Medium
Drumsticks	1 lb	1 hour	Medium
Hindquarters	3 lbs	1¼ hours	Medium
Thighs	1½ lb	1 hour	Medium
Patties	¾ inch	15 min	Med–Hot

FISH

Fish of various types and sizes requires different cooking times, and it's difficult to establish a chart as such. There is a rule of thumb, however, that will help.

I suggest using a basket that has been brushed with oil. Watch the fish closely, as most fish will cook in a matter of minutes. If the total weight of what you are cooking is in the 1 to 1½ pounds range, the cooking time will be approximately 15 to 20 minutes. Turn the fish over about 7 or 8 minutes into the cooking. This is the rule. If the fish flakes with a fork, it's done.

INDIRECT GRILLING

Indirect grilling is done on a covered grill, usually with a drip pan with an inch or so of water in it. I have found the average cooking heat to be in the medium range directly above the heat source. This will provide for a medium-low heat above the drip pan. The medium-low heat will allow slow, natural tenderizing of the meat and help keep the flavor in and the meat moist.

This type cooking takes longer than direct grilling and one must remember to keep an eye on the heat source. You must maintain a constant heat and not allow it to get too low. If you are using a gas grilling device, you shouldn't have any problem unless you run out of gas. Always check the amount of gas before you start grilling sizable chunks of meat. I can't relate the sorrow that goes with having to finish a nice roast in an oven.

I have tried to determine a cooking time per pound of meat being grilled and have come up with this. There are just too many variables to be accurate. The size, cut, fat content, bone in or out, and doneness desired are a few of the things to determine. That is why I suggest a meat thermometer be used until you have established a natural ability to judge the doneness of your food. I sometimes use one and I've been cooking for years.

Stick the thermometer deep into the thickest part of the meat, making sure it does not touch any bones. Remember to turn the thermometer so it can be easily seen so you don't have to have the grill opened too long and allow heat loss.

DONENESS TEMPERATURES

BEEF

	140 degrees	Rare
	160 degrees	Medium
	170 degrees	Well

PORK

	170 degrees (always cook pork well)	Well-Done

FULLY COOKED HAMS

140 degrees (Since it has already been cooked, you want to heat it to allow the flavor to cook in, but you don't want to overcook it.)

LAMB

The same temperatures used for beef can be used for lamb.

Poultry should be grilled over medium heat above the drip pan. This will require a medium-hot heat source that must be maintained. Indirect grilling is usually reserved for grilling whole birds such as chicken, turkey, pheasant, quail, cornish game hens, and others.

Again, there is a problem in relating a specific time for grilling individual types of birds. A good rule of thumb would be this.

WHOLE CHICKENS-PHEASANTS-QUAIL-GAME HENS

To test for doneness, grip the end of the drumstick. (I don't have to tell you to use something to keep from getting burned, do I?) The drumstick should move up and down easily and twist in the socket.

TURKEYS

Stick a meat thermometer into the middle of the inside of the thigh muscle. Don't let it touch the bone. When it registers 180 degrees, it should be done. If you are doing just a full breast, 170 degrees.

"You never get a second chance at making a first impression." I don't know who I just quoted, but it seems to fit in right now. Making the right impression is easy for the true pitman.

1. Don't get this book out for information in front of guests.
2. Act relaxed like everything is just matter of fact.
3. Have everything in place before guests start showing up.
4. Unless you are cooking something that requires a great deal of time, don't start the fire until the guests get there. And be sure to stress the need for the heat to be just right.
5. Above all others, make sure you have an extra piece to grill as a "Cook's Sample." This shows them you like your own cooking, but it also lets you see how things are doing.
6. Enjoy yourself and have a good time. That's what barbecuing is all about.

JUST SOME
THOUGHTS

As you might have guessed by now, I like to cook. I also have a thing for old cookbooks and recipes. Over the years I have had several people complain about an old recipe their Grandmother had that didn't turn out. I have found a lot of these recipes in many of my old books and finally figured out why they didn't work. Most of the old books were written with different measurements.

Here is a conversion list I put together to help out those who might find a "Good ol' Good One" but are afraid to try it.

NEW VERSION	OLD VERSION
3 tsp	1 tbsp
2 tbsp	1 fluid oz
4 tbsp	¼ cup
6 tbsp	⅜ cup
8 tbsp	½ cup
16 tbsp	1 cup
1 cup	8 fluid oz
2 cups	1 pint
2 pints	1 quart
4 qts	1 gal
1 peck	2 gal
4 pecks	1 bu
16 oz	1 lb
2 cups liquid	1 lb
4 cups flour	1 lb
2 cups granulated sugar	1 lb

(continued on next page)

NEW VERSION	OLD VERSION
2⅔ cups brown sugar	1 lb
3½ cups powdered sugar	1 lb
2 cups butter	1 lb
2 cups solid meat	1 lb
4 tbsp flour	1 oz
2 tsp butter or salt	1 oz

Another thing that I am often asked is about spices. So many people find old family recipes and don't know how to make it because of the ingredients. If they don't know what something is, they don't try the dish. Don't let this stop your efforts. You may be missing something great. To help with this problem, I will list a few items and what they do.

Let's start with herbs

BAY LEAVES—These are particularly good in about any meat dish you might be making. Try some of these when you create your own sauces. (WARNING: Do not overuse bay leaves; a little goes a long way.)

CHERVIL—This herb is a lot like parsley but milder. Young leaves may be used in meat dishes and in sauces. (NOTICE: This herb is also known as FINES HERBS when in a powdered state.)

DILL—Dill seeds and leaves are used. Use the leaves as a garnish or to cook with fish. Try some dill juice from a jar of pickles when a recipe for barbecue sauce calls for vinegar. It makes for a nice change.

FENNEL—This herb has a sweet hot-flavor. Seeds are more commonly used in very small quantities in pie, etc. Leaves may be boiled with fish.

I like to poach some fish in water with this and then add a good vinegar-based sauce at the table.

MARJORAM—This may be used in both the green or dry stage for flavoring soups and sauces. This makes a very nice secret ingredient for stuffings for meat or fish.

MINT—Use crushed mint in salads, teas, meat sauces, and as an addition to sweet barbecue sauces.

PARSLEY—Without a doubt one of the most popular herbs used ever. There is no stopping this herb. Soups, salads, gravies and especially barbecue sauce can be enhanced by parsley. Sprinkle a little chopped parsley on anything you barbecued along with your table sauce, I think you'll like it.

SAGE—Used fresh or dried. This herb is especially good when used in small amounts with any type meat or poultry. Mix a little dried sage in your rub for a delightfully different taste. (NOTE: I don't like sage with any boiled or poached fish. A little sprinkled on fried or grilled fish, such as trout, is refreshing. WARNING: Don't over use. This can be a very strong herb.)

SAVORY—This herb has a very agreeable flavor and blends well with other flavors. Great in sauces, soups and stuffings.

SWEET BASIL—Distinct flavor of cloves. Use lightly with meats and sauces.

TARRAGON—Leaves have a hot, pungent taste. Use in sauces. Tarragon also can be used to flavor vinegar. Another source for a new taste in a barbecue sauce.

THYME—Leaves or ground. This herb works well with sauces and meat. Add a little to your rub.

Seeds

CARDAMON—Flavor is especially good with honey mixtures like sauces. Add a little to your sauce.

CURRY POWDER—This is simply a blend of spices combined to give a distinct flavor. (WARNING: Use in small amounts for meat or fish. Add a little to your rub.)

MACE—Actually a part of the nutmeg seed. Can be used in sauces. (WARNING: Mace is also used in some pickles so read label on jar before adding additional mace to your sauce if you are using pickle juice.)

MUSTARD—Dry mustard works very well in most meat sauces.

PAPRIKA—This is a Hungarian red pepper. May be used in all meat dishes and sauces. Also a good garnish for side dishes.

PEPPER, BLACK—Comes from ground peppercorn. Used with anything except sweets.

PEPPER, CAYENNE—A derivative of capsicum. Dull red color and should be used in small amounts for those with a tender palate. (WARNING: HOT! Best stored in refrigeration if not totally used in a short time. Larva will grow in cayenne. If you notice a web-type condition in your cayenne, simply place pepper in fridge)

So now you have decided to have a few friends over for a cookout. But how much will you need? This is a quick rule of thumb guide I hope will help.

FOR 25 GUESTS

FOOD	SERVINGS
SANDWICHES	
Bread	3, 1 lb loaves
Butter	½ lb
Mayonnaise	1 cup
Lettuce	2 heads
MEAT, POULTRY, OR FISH	
Weiners	6½ lbs
Hamburger	9 lbs
Ham (sliced)	12 lbs
Turkey or Chicken	13 lbs
Fish (fillets)	7½ lbs
SALADS	
Potato Salad	4½ qts
Slaw	2 qts
Baked Beans	1 gal
ICE CREAM	
Bulk	3 gal
BEVERAGES	3½ gal
WATERMELON	40 lbs

Double the amounts for every 25 guests. I didn't leave out other meats, I just have a different rule for that. If you are going to grill large portions of meat for a cookout, figure at least one pound of raw meat per person. Remember the meat will reduce in size as it cooks. So when it's done you should have about ¾ pound per person.

INDEX

V

Y

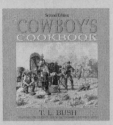